CW00417650

CELEBRATING THE MANY FACES OF DAWN FRENCH

A Biography written by:

MAURIE PUTELLA

All rights reserved. No part of this publication may be reproduced, distributed, or transmitted in any form or by any means, including photocopying, recording, or other electronic or mechanical methods, without the prior written permission of the publisher, except in the case of brief quotations embodied in critical reviews and certain other noncommercial uses permitted by copyright law.

Copyright © 2023, Maurie Putella.

TABLE OF CONTENTS

PREFACE

Dawn Roma French, born on the 11th of October, 1957, is a celebrated figure in the world of British entertainment. Her multifaceted talents encompass acting, comedy, presenting, and writing, rendering her a revered presence in the industry. French's remarkable career includes a plethora of accomplishments that have left an indelible mark on British comedy and television.

One of her most iconic partnerships was forged with her closest confidante and comedic counterpart, Jennifer Saunders. Together, they crafted the uproarious BBC comedy sketch show, aptly titled "French and Saunders." This show served as a veritable comedic playground where their wit and humor dazzled audiences, leaving them in stitches with each sketch and character portrayal. The collaborative chemistry they shared was nothing short of magical, and their comedic genius resonated with viewers far and wide.

However, Dawn French's talents extended well beyond sketch comedy. She ventured into the world of sitcoms with a performance that remains etched in the annals of British television history. In the beloved BBC sitcom "The Vicar of Dibley," she assumed the leading role of Geraldine Granger. Her portrayal of the charismatic and unconventional vicar endeared her to audiences and catapulted her to even greater stardom.

French's contributions to the world of entertainment have not gone unnoticed by the industry itself. Her exceptional talent has earned her a staggering seven nominations for the prestigious BAFTA TV Awards, a testament to her prowess as a performer. Yet, her accolades don't stop there. In 2009, she achieved the pinnacle of recognition when she and her comedic partner, Jennifer Saunders, were honored with a BAFTA Fellowship. This esteemed award not only acknowledged their immeasurable impact on the world of comedy but also celebrated their enduring friendship and creative partnership.

As we delve into the tapestry of Dawn French's career, we find a remarkable individual who has brought laughter and joy to countless lives. Her talents are an integral part of the British comedic landscape, and her legacy as a writer, actress, and comedian is destined to endure for generations to come.

EARLY LIFE AND
BACKGROUND

In the realm of early life, Dawn Roma French's story unfolds against the backdrop of Holyhead, Wales, where she came into the world on the 11th of October in 1957. Her birthright was a blend of Welsh and English heritage, as her parents, Felicity Roma (née O'Brien) and Denys Vernon French, hailed from England. This union of hearts occurred in their hometown of Plymouth, back in 1953, and it set the stage for Dawn's unique journey.

Within the framework of her family, Dawn shared her upbringing with an older brother named Gary. Their familial tapestry was woven with threads of adventure, thanks to her father's service in the Royal Air Force. Denys French's military career took the family to diverse locations, including RAF Valley and later RAF Leconfield. It was during this time that an enchanting moment unfolded when Queen Elizabeth The Queen Mother graced the French family home with her presence, all when young Dawn was a mere three years old. The remarkable memory of this royal visit was preserved in RAF archive footage and later became a charming chapter in Dawn's comedy tour and video, "Thirty Million Minutes."

The Royal Air Force played a pivotal role not only in their family's journey but also in Dawn's educational path. The RAF provided partial funding for her private education, an opportunity that paved the way for her intellectual growth. During her father's posting at RAF Faldingworth, Dawn attended Caistor Grammar School for a brief period, immersing herself in the world of learning.

However, her educational journey was far from ordinary. Dawn's thirst for knowledge and ambition led her across the Atlantic to the vibrant city of New York. Here, she embarked on a transformative chapter by enrolling at the prestigious Spence School. This decision was no whimsy; it was a result of her remarkable talent as a debater, earning her a coveted scholarship during her school days.

As she ventured across the ocean and into the hallowed halls of the Spence School, Dawn's horizons broadened even further. This period of her life not only enriched her intellect but also laid the foundation for the incredible journey she would undertake in the world of comedy and entertainment.

Dawn French's remarkable journey through life was significantly influenced by her father, a man whose words and love instilled within her an unwavering self-confidence and self-belief. Each day, he would tell her how beautiful she was, nurturing her sense of self-worth. Dawn herself fondly recalled this pivotal aspect of her upbringing, stating, "He taught me to value myself. He told me that I was beautiful and the most precious thing in his life." Her father's boundless support and affirmation left an indelible mark on her, shaping her into the strong and confident individual she would become.

However, beneath this facade of strength, her father, Denys, harbored a hidden battle with severe depression. Despite his inner turmoil, he managed to shield his suffering from Dawn and her brother, Gary. The depth of his anguish remained concealed, a heavy secret that he carried.

Tragedy struck when Dawn was just nineteen years old, as her father, Denys, succumbed to the grip of depression and ended his life by suicide. This devastating loss marked a profound turning point in Dawn's life, casting a long shadow of grief over her path.

In the midst of this emotional turmoil, Dawn French embarked on a new chapter in 1977 when she enrolled in drama studies at the Royal Central School of Speech and Drama. Little did she know that within these hallowed halls, she would encounter her future comedic partner, Jennifer Saunders. Interestingly, both Dawn and Jennifer shared a common thread in their backgrounds—the RAF. They had grown up on the same base, even sharing the same best friend, although they had never crossed paths until this pivotal moment.

Their initial impressions of each other were less than harmonious. Dawn, exuding confidence and determination, might have appeared as a "cocky little upstart" to Saunders. Conversely, Dawn found Saunders to be somewhat snooty and aloof. Their initial clash of personalities stemmed from differing aspirations; Dawn harbored dreams of becoming a drama teacher, while Saunders harbored a vehement aversion to the idea, thereby disliking Dawn for her enthusiasm and confidence in pursuing this course.

Little did they know that this initial friction would eventually evolve into one of the most dynamic and iconic comedic partnerships in British entertainment history.

As destiny would have it, Dawn French and Jennifer Saunders found themselves sharing a flat during their college days. It was here, within the confines of their student accommodation, that their comedic destinies were profoundly influenced. Their flatmates, as part of their college projects, delved into the world of comedy, unwittingly laying the groundwork for what would become a legendary partnership.

Although they had coexisted in the same living space, it was during one candid and in-depth conversation that the sparks of friendship truly ignited between Dawn and Jennifer. Their connection deepened as they shared their dreams, aspirations, and a mutual love for the art of comedy.

However, college life had its own set of trials. During this period, Dawn French experienced the end of a significant relationship, parting ways with her fiancé, who happened to be a former Royal Navy officer. This transition, marked by heartbreak and personal growth, would prove pivotal in shaping her future path.

Upon their graduation from the Royal Central School of Speech and Drama, the dynamic duo made a momentous decision: to join forces and create a double-act named the "Menopause Sisters." The moniker might raise an eyebrow today, but it aptly captured their audacious and unconventional comedic style. Their early acts even featured the eyebrow-raising visual gag of wearing tampons in their ears, a choice Jennifer Saunders later described as "cringeworthy." Their initial foray into the comedy scene didn't exactly exude "star quality," as one club manager recalled, but it was a humble beginning that would soon lead to greater things.

Dawn French and Jennifer Saunders began to make waves in the public eye as integral members of the Comic Strip, a collective that emerged within the vibrant alternative comedy scene of the early 1980s. Their talent and unique comedic flair were slowly but surely garnering attention, setting the stage for their ascent into the comedic pantheon.

PERSONAL LIFE AND CHALLENGES

Marriage, Family And Personal Relationships

In her personal life, Dawn French's journey took an intriguing turn when she crossed paths with fellow comedian Lenny Henry within the vibrant realm of the alternative comedy circuit. Their connection was not merely comedic; it blossomed into a deep and enduring romantic relationship. On the 20th of October in 1984, the couple sealed their love with a wedding ceremony in the heart of Covent Garden, London. Their union marked a significant chapter in both their lives, blending their comedic talents with a shared journey in the world of entertainment.

As their love story evolved, Dawn and Lenny decided to expand their family through adoption, welcoming a daughter named Billie into their lives. From the outset, transparency was a fundamental principle in their family. Billie was always aware of her adoptive status, and her parents ensured she grew up with this knowledge.

However, the couple faced a challenging moment when a biographer threatened to unveil the identity of Billie's biological mother. Dawn, fiercely protective of her family's privacy, took legal action by obtaining an injunction to safeguard Billie's personal history. When questioned about the prospect of Billie wanting to explore her birth mother's identity in the future, Dawn's response reflected her unwavering support and respect for her daughter's autonomy. She expressed, "Whatever she wants to do when she's 18, we'll support her. What I do worry about is anyone else making the decision for her." This unwavering commitment to Billie's choices underscored the strength of their familial bond.

Beyond her family life, Dawn French's engagement extended to the realm of politics. During the 2010 general election campaign, she was cited as a supporter of the Labour Party, aligning herself with their political ideals. Her advocacy for the party continued, as she threw her support behind Keir Starmer during the 2020 Labour leadership election. In doing so, she leveraged her platform to champion the causes and leaders she believed in, a testament to her commitment to societal and political change.

In her personal life, Dawn French's journey took an intriguing turn when she crossed paths with fellow comedian Lenny Henry within the vibrant realm of the alternative comedy circuit. Their connection was not merely comedic; it blossomed into a deep and enduring romantic relationship. On the 20th of October in 1984, the couple sealed their love with a wedding ceremony in the heart of Covent Garden, London. Their union marked a significant chapter in both their lives, blending their comedic talents with a shared journey in the world of entertainment.

As their love story evolved, Dawn and Lenny decided to expand their family through adoption, welcoming a daughter named Billie into their lives. From the outset, transparency was a fundamental principle in their family. Billie was always aware of her adoptive status, and her parents ensured she grew up with this knowledge.

However, the couple faced a challenging moment when a biographer threatened to unveil the identity of Billie's biological mother. Dawn, fiercely protective of her family's privacy, took legal action by obtaining an injunction to safeguard Billie's personal history. When questioned about the prospect of Billie wanting to explore her birth mother's identity in the future, Dawn's response reflected her unwavering support and respect for her daughter's autonomy. She expressed, "Whatever she wants to do when she's 18, we'll support her. What I do worry about is anyone else making the decision for her." This unwavering commitment to Billie's choices underscored the strength of their familial bond.

Beyond her family life, Dawn French's engagement extended to the realm of politics. During the 2010 general election campaign, she was cited as a supporter of the Labour Party, aligning herself with their political ideals. Her advocacy for the party continued, as she threw her support behind Keir Starmer during the 2020 Labour leadership election. In doing so, she leveraged her platform to champion the causes and leaders she believed in, a testament to her commitment to societal and political change.

A RISING STAR

In the dynamic realm of 1980s television, Dawn French made her memorable debut on the small screen. Her television journey commenced in 1982 when she graced the screens as part of Channel 4's "The Comic Strip Presents" series. This series was a tapestry of self-contained stories, and in this creative milieu, alongside her comedic partner Jennifer Saunders, French showcased her comedic brilliance. The ensemble cast also featured an array of talented Comic Strip performers, including luminaries such as Peter Richardson, Rik Mayall, Nigel Planer, Robbie Coltrane, and Adrian Edmondson. Dawn's involvement in this series was substantial, as she not only acted in a staggering 27 out of the 37 episodes but also demonstrated her aptitude for comedy writing by contributing to the creation of two episodes.

Within this eclectic series, viewers were treated to a diverse range of comedic gems. One episode stood out as a clever parody of spaghetti westerns, while another transported audiences to the whimsical world of a black and white film, where a hopelessly goofy boy took center stage. These episodes exemplified Dawn French's versatility and comedic prowess, showcasing her ability to breathe life into an array of characters and scenarios.

A pivotal moment in expanding her audience came in 1981 when comedy producer Martin Lewis recorded a Comic Strip record album. This album, released on Springtime!/Island Records in September 1981, featured sketches by none other than French and Jennifer Saunders. This marked their first introduction to an audience beyond the confines of London, serving as a precursor to their meteoric rise in the world of comedy.

In 1985, Dawn French continued to make her mark on television as she joined forces with Jennifer Saunders, Tracey Ullman, and Ruby Wax in the series "Girls on Top." This comedy portrayed the quirky and endearing lives of four eccentric women sharing a flat in the bustling heart of London, offering a fresh perspective on female-centric humor.

The 1980s were a formative period in Dawn French's television career, where she honed her craft, displayed her comedic versatility, and left an indelible mark on the world of entertainment.

The 2000s saw Dawn French continue to captivate audiences with her versatile acting skills and comedic charm on television.

In 2002, she graced the screen in the comedy/drama mini-series titled "Ted and Alice." Set amidst the picturesque backdrop of the Lake District, French took on the role of a tourist information officer who embarks on a truly unconventional romantic journey—falling in love with an alien. This quirky and imaginative series allowed French to showcase her comedic and dramatic talents in equal measure, blending humor with elements of heartfelt storytelling.

Dawn French made a memorable guest appearance in the iconic sitcom "Absolutely Fabulous" in 1992. In this role, she portrayed TV interviewer Kathy, offering a hilarious parody of the well-known television personality Lorraine Kelly. Her performance left a lasting impression, and she had the opportunity to reprise this role in "Absolutely Fabulous: The Movie" in 2016, where Kathy had evolved into a seasoned veteran journalist, mirroring Kelly's real-life career trajectory.

Additionally, French's television ventures led her to the BBC sitcom "Wild West," where she shared the screen with the talented Catherine Tate. In this series, she portrayed a character living in Cornwall, navigating the complexities of her life as a lesbian, a situation more driven by circumstances than any innate inclination. While this series explored themes with sensitivity and humor, it did not attain the same level of success as some of her earlier roles and concluded in 2004 after a two-year run.

Throughout the 2000s, Dawn French continued to diversify her television portfolio, effortlessly transitioning between comedic and dramatic roles, all the while leaving an indelible mark on the small screen.

The 2000s continued to be a prolific period for Dawn French on television, as she took on a variety of roles, showcasing her versatility as an actress.

In the series "Jam & Jerusalem," French assumed a major role as Rosie, a character grappling with dissociative identity disorder. Within this condition, Rosie harbored an alter ego named "Margaret." This complex portrayal allowed French to delve into the intricacies of mental health and identity. She shared the screen with an ensemble cast that included Sue Johnston, Jennifer Saunders (who also created and wrote the series), and Joanna

Lumley, adding depth to the series with her performance.

A memorable guest appearance for French came in the popular sketch show "Little Britain," where she portrayed Vicky Pollard's mother, adding her comedic touch to the show's quirky characters. In a special edition of "Little Britain Live," presented as part of Comic Relief, French's comedic talents shone as she played a lesbian barmaid in a sketch alongside the flamboyant character Daffyd Thomas.

In 2006, French graced the screen in "Agatha Christie's Marple," taking on a role in the episode titled "Sleeping Murder." Her appearance in this beloved mystery series showcased her adaptability in a different genre, further cementing her reputation as a versatile actress.

One of her notable roles in 2008 was in the BBC television drama "Lark Rise to Candleford," where she portrayed Caroline Arless. Her character was described as vibrant and extreme, a woman who lived life to the fullest, often indulging in laughter, singing, and perhaps a bit too much drinking. Despite her character's quirks, French's portrayal emphasized the deep love Caroline had for her family, adding depth and authenticity to the role.

Throughout the 2000s, Dawn French continued to leave her mark on television, seamlessly transitioning between a range of characters and genres, all while delivering memorable performances that resonated with audiences.

Music videos

Dawn French's presence extended to the realm of music videos, where she added her unique charm and humor to various memorable productions.

In 1986, she made an appearance in Kate Bush's music video for "Experiment IV." In this visually captivating video, she shared the screen with notable figures like Hugh Laurie, Richard Vernon, and Peter Vaughan, contributing her distinctive presence to the project.

Her collaboration with singer Alison Moyet resulted in appearances in two of Moyet's music videos. In 1987, she featured in the video for "Love Letters," a song that also included her comedic partner Jennifer Saunders. The duo's chemistry added an entertaining element to the music video. In 1994, French returned to Moyet's music video for "Whispering Your Name," once again showcasing her talent for enhancing visual storytelling with her presence.

Dawn French's commitment to charitable causes also extended to the world of music. In 1989, she, Jennifer Saunders, and Kathy Burke formed the musical ensemble Lananeeneenoonoo. Along with Bananarama, they collaborated on a charity single to raise funds for Comic Relief. Their cover version of The Beatles' classic "Help!" not only entertained but also contributed to a noble cause, making a significant impact on the UK Singles Chart and the hearts of those who supported the charity.

French, Saunders, and Burke continued their involvement with Comic Relief in 1997 as "The Sugar Lumps." Alongside Llewella Gideon and Lulu, they parodied The Spice Girls and collaborated with the original group on a version of "Who Do You Think You Are?" Their humorous take on the iconic song delighted fans and further solidified their involvement in charitable endeavors through music.

Dawn French's appearances in music videos added an entertaining dimension to her diverse career, showcasing her ability to bring her comedic talent to different artistic mediums.

THE COMIC PARTNERSHIP

Meeting Jennifer Saunders

In the annals of comedy, Dawn French's collaboration with Jennifer Saunders stands as an iconic testament to their creative genius. Together, they co-wrote and starred in the groundbreaking comedy series "French & Saunders," which made its debut in 1987. This was a show that redefined the landscape of humor and introduced an unforgettable array of celebrity spoofs and cinematic parodies that continue to resonate with audiences.

Within the playful confines of "French & Saunders," the dynamic duo fearlessly lampooned a multitude of celebrities. Their comedic prowess knew no bounds as they took on the personas of pop culture icons like Madonna, Cher, Catherine Zeta-Jones, and even the irrepressible Spice Girls. With impeccable mimicry and a keen eye for satire, French and Saunders breathed life into these famous figures, turning their quirks and idiosyncrasies into a source of endless laughter.

Yet, their comedic repertoire extended far beyond celebrity caricatures. In a stroke of genius, they ventured into the realm of film parody, fearlessly tackling beloved cinematic classics. "The Lord of the Rings," "Star Wars," and "Harry Potter and the Chamber of Secrets" all fell under their satirical scrutiny. With a remarkable blend of wit, humor, and an undeniable love for the source material, they reimagined these epic tales through their unique comedic lens, delivering a fresh and uproarious take on these cinematic masterpieces.

Their unparalleled partnership in "French & Saunders" continued to flourish for two glorious decades, serving as a constant source of delight for viewers. However, even after this extended run, their comedic journey was far from over. In 2007, they rekindled the magic with their sketch series titled "A Bucket o' French & Saunders," reaffirming their status as comedic legends. Premiering on the 8th of September that year, this series demonstrated that their comedic brilliance remained as vibrant and relevant as ever.

Throughout their remarkable career together, Dawn French and Jennifer Saunders shaped the landscape of comedy with their wit, satire, and fearless approach to humor. Their enduring legacy is a testament to their boundless creativity and their ability to bring laughter and joy to countless lives.

The birth of "French and Saunders"

In the dynamic realm of 1980s television, Dawn French made her memorable debut on the small screen. Her television journey commenced in 1982 when she graced the screens as part of Channel 4's "The Comic Strip Presents" series. This series was a tapestry of self-contained stories, and in this creative milieu, alongside her comedic partner Jennifer Saunders, French showcased her comedic brilliance. The ensemble cast also featured an array of talented Comic Strip performers, including luminaries such as Peter Richardson, Rik Mayall, Nigel Planer, Robbie Coltrane, and Adrian Edmondson. Dawn's involvement in this series was substantial, as she not only acted in a staggering 27 out of the 37 episodes but also demonstrated her aptitude for comedy writing by contributing to the creation of two episodes.

Within this eclectic series, viewers were treated to a diverse range of comedic gems. One episode stood out as a clever parody of spaghetti westerns, while another transported audiences to the whimsical world of a black and white film, where a hopelessly goofy boy took center stage. These episodes exemplified Dawn French's versatility and comedic prowess, showcasing her ability to breathe life into an array of characters and scenarios.

A pivotal moment in expanding her audience came in 1981 when comedy producer Martin Lewis recorded a Comic Strip record album. This album, released on Springtime!/Island Records in September 1981, featured sketches by none other than French and Jennifer Saunders. This marked their first introduction to an audience beyond the confines of London, serving as a precursor to their meteoric rise in the world of comedy.

In 1985, Dawn French continued to make her mark on television as she joined forces with Jennifer Saunders, Tracey Ullman, and Ruby Wax in the series "Girls on Top." This comedy portrayed the quirky and endearing lives of four eccentric women sharing a flat in the bustling heart of London, offering a fresh perspective on female-centric humor.

The 1980s were a formative period in Dawn French's television career, where she honed her craft, displayed her comedic versatility, and left an indelible mark on the world of entertainment.

LEGACIES OF DAWN FRENCH

As the 2010s dawned, Dawn French continued to grace television screens with her undeniable talent and charisma.

In late 2010, she took on a starring role in the series "Roger & Val Have Just Got In," alongside actor Alfred Molina. The show, which aired for two series, provided viewers with an intimate look into the lives of a couple navigating the ordinary yet often humorous challenges of everyday life.

In a festive treat for audiences, French appeared in "Little Crackers," a series of short comedy films broadcast during the Christmas season in 2010. These heartwarming and humorous tales added a touch of laughter and merriment to the holiday season.

In December 2011, French was a special guest on "Michael Bublé's Home For Christmas," sharing the joy of the season with audiences alongside the celebrated crooner Michael Bublé.

July 2012 saw her take on the role of a judge in ITV's "Superstar" live shows, bringing her expertise and unique perspective to the talent competition.

In March 2013, an exciting international opportunity came her way, as French joined the judging panel of Nine Network's "Australia's Got Talent." Alongside fellow judges Kyle Sandilands, Geri Halliwell (who replaced Dannii Minogue), and Timomatic, she brought her discerning eye and charismatic presence to the show. However, she departed after one series, making way for Kelly Osbourne.

From 2016 to 2019, Dawn French embarked on a captivating journey in the series "Delicious," which aired on Sky 1. In this culinary drama, she played a talented cook entangled in a complex web of love, secrets, and rivalries. Her character found herself in an affair with her celebrity chef ex-husband, portrayed by Iain Glen, who had moved on to a successful hotel business with his new wife, played by Emilia Fox. Against the scenic backdrop of Cornwall, this series explored the intricacies of relationships, ambition, and the world of gastronomy.

Throughout the 2010s, Dawn French's television career continued to evolve, offering audiences a diverse range of roles and experiences that showcased her enduring talent and magnetism on the small screen.

The 2020s brought a fresh wave of television appearances for the ever-talented Dawn French.

In 2020, she graced screens in the six-part series "The Trouble with Maggie Cole," where she shared the spotlight with actor Mark Heap. This engaging series provided viewers with a compelling narrative, further cementing French's status as a prominent figure in the world of television.

Continuing her journey in the world of entertainment, Dawn French made a notable guest appearance as a celebrity judge on the second series of "RuPaul's Drag Race UK" in 2021. In this role, she brought her discerning eye and comedic flair to the competition, where she evaluated the final five contestants. As they showcased their comedic stand-up routines, French's presence added a touch of star power to the show, making for a memorable and entertaining episode.

The 2020s found Dawn French as vibrant and relevant as ever, gracing television screens with her charisma and talent, and leaving her mark on some of the most exciting and diverse shows of the era.

BEYOND COMEDY

Exploring Diverse Roles in Film and Television
Dawn French's talent extended beyond television, and she made a significant impact in the world of film as well.

In 1996, she graced the silver screen in "The Adventures of Pinocchio," where she portrayed "The Baker's Wife." This film, featuring notable actors like Martin Landau and Jonathan Taylor Thomas, allowed French to bring her charm to the enchanting world of this classic story.

Her cinematic journey also took her to the magical universe of "Harry Potter." In the film adaptation of "Harry Potter and the Prisoner of Azkaban," she portrayed "The Fat Lady," a character whose persona she took over from Elizabeth Spriggs, who had played the role in the first film of the series. Interestingly, her then-husband, Lenny Henry, lent his voice to the character of the Shrunken Head in the same film, though they didn't share screen time.

In 2005, French ventured into the realm of voice acting, providing her distinct voice to the character Mrs. Beaver in Disney and Walden Media's adaptation of C.S. Lewis' timeless classic, "The Chronicles of Narnia: The Lion, the Witch and the Wardrobe." Her voice added depth and personality to this beloved character.

In 2010, French's voice talent shone once more as she lent her voice to the character Angie the Elephant in the English dub of the German-British environmental animated film "Animals United." Her contributions enhanced the film's appeal to English-speaking audiences.

Dawn French's foray into the world of film showcased her versatility as an actress and voice artist, allowing her to leave her mark on some of the most beloved stories and characters in cinematic history.

Life in Theatre

Dawn French's artistic talents extended to the realm of theater, where she brought her charisma and skill to the live stage in various productions.

One of her notable theater roles included appearing in the enchanting world of William Shakespeare's "A Midsummer Night's Dream." Her performance in this timeless play added a new dimension to the beloved characters and the magic of Shakespearean theater.

In "My Brilliant Divorce," another theatrical endeavor, French delivered a captivating portrayal that showcased her range as an actress. Her ability to embody complex characters and convey their emotions resonated with theater audiences.

In "Smaller," she took on the role of a devoted schoolteacher caring for her disabled mother. This poignant and emotionally charged play allowed French to explore the depths of her acting prowess, delivering a moving performance that left a lasting impact on audiences.

January 2007 marked a momentous occasion as Dawn French graced the stage of the Royal Opera House, Covent Garden, London. In this grand venue, she took on the role of the Duchesse de Crackentorp in "The Daughter of the Regiment" (La fille du régiment) by Gaetano Donizetti. Her participation in this operatic production, alongside stars like Natalie Dessay and Juan Diego Flórez, was a testament to her versatility as an artist.

Her connection to Covent Garden continued as she returned for the 2010 revival of "La Fille du règiment," reprising her role in this beloved opera.

Most recently, in December 2022, Dawn French graced the London Palladium stage in "Jack and the Beanstalk," adding another chapter to her rich theatrical career. Her presence on stage continued to captivate and delight audiences, reaffirming her status as a dynamic and beloved performer across various artistic mediums.

THE LATER YEARS LEGACIES AND IMPACTS

Dawn French's comedic brilliance also found expression in the world of stand-up comedy, where she connected with audiences through her unique brand of humor.

In 2014, she embarked on a captivating journey with her autobiographical one-woman show titled "30 Million Minutes." The title of the show was a clever nod to the number of minutes she had lived up to that point in her life, offering audiences a glimpse into her personal experiences and insights. This intimate and engaging performance took her on a tour across the UK and Oceania, allowing fans to connect with her on a more personal level and sharing in her life's moments of laughter and reflection.

In 2022, French returned to the stand-up comedy stage with a new show titled "Dawn French is a Huge Twat." This humorous title hinted at the irreverent and witty humor audiences could expect from her performance. Her tour across the UK was met with enthusiasm, as fans eagerly gathered to witness her comedic prowess in action.

Excitingly, in late 2022, it was announced that Dawn French would continue to tour the UK with the same show in Autumn 2023, extending the opportunity for more audiences to enjoy her comedy. Furthermore, plans were set for shows in Australia in 2024, promising to bring her unique brand of humor to an international audience.

Through her stand-up comedy, Dawn French continued to connect with fans, sharing laughter and insights from her life's journey, and proving that her comedic talent remained as sharp and relevant as ever.

The Advertising world

Dawn French's captivating presence and charm also made her a sought-after figure in the world of advertising, where she lent her talents to various campaigns.

From 1997 until August 2007, French was the face of Terry's Chocolate Orange, becoming synonymous with the delightful treat. Her association with this iconic confectionery brand added a touch of warmth and humor to their advertisements, leaving a lasting impression on audiences.

Additionally, she graced screens in commercials for the Churchill Insurance Company, where her charismatic presence and distinctive voice made a memorable impact.

In 2019, Dawn French provided her voice for numerous station idents for Greatest Hits Radio, collaborating with Bespoke Music to create a distinctive auditory experience for the radio network.

In 2021, French took on a delightful role as the voice of a fairy lady for the Christmas food advertisements of leading retailer Marks and Spencer. In this heartwarming campaign, she shared the stage with Tom Holland, who voiced the company's beloved mascot, Percy Pig. French's character, the fairy, drops her magic wand onto a box adorned with Percy Pig wrappings, bringing Percy to life for the first time in 29 years. Throughout the advertisement, she showcases the array of Christmas food items available from the retailer, creating a sense of magic and festivity.

Continuing her association with Marks and Spencer, she reprised the role for the 2022 M&S Christmas advert, where she was joined by her comedic partner Jennifer Saunders, who voiced a sidekick character named 'Duckie.' Together, they embarked on a journey to fill Duckie with festive cheer while highlighting the M&S Food Christmas range for 2022.

Dawn French's contributions to the world of advertising added humor, warmth, and a touch of magic to various campaigns, making her a beloved figure in the realm of commercial endorsements.

Awards And Recognition

Dawn French's talent and contributions to the world of entertainment have not gone unnoticed, and she has received several awards and accolades for her outstanding work.

In 2002, French and her comedy partner, Jennifer Saunders, were honored with the prestigious Golden Rose of Montreux award, recognizing their exceptional contributions to comedy. This acknowledgment celebrated their comedic brilliance and their enduring impact on the world of entertainment.

In 2003, Dawn French was recognized as one of the 50 funniest acts in British comedy by The Observer, a testament to her enduring popularity and her status as a comedic icon in the UK.

A 2006 poll involving 4,000 people affirmed French's place in the hearts of the British public, as she was named the most admired female celebrity among women in Britain. This widespread admiration attested to her relatability and the connection she forged with her audience.

In February 2013, Dawn French received recognition of a different kind, as she was assessed as one of the 100 most powerful women in the United Kingdom by Woman's Hour on BBC Radio 4. This acknowledgment showcased her influence and significance not only in the entertainment industry but also as a prominent figure in British society.

Dawn French's awards and recognition reflect the profound impact she has made on the world of comedy and entertainment, solidifying her status as a beloved and influential figure in the hearts and minds of audiences in the UK and beyond.

THE CREATIVE GENIUS

Dawn French is not only a gifted actress and comedian but also a talented writer, with a diverse range of literary works to her credit.

In 2008, she penned her best-selling autobiography, "Dear Fatty," which takes the form of an epistolary narrative. The title is a playful reference to her close friend and comedic partner, Jennifer Saunders, with whom she shares a long and enduring friendship. French was granted a substantial £1.5 million advance for the book, which offered readers a candid and heartfelt glimpse into her life. Through a series of letters addressed to various people who have played significant roles in her life, she shared her personal journey, making it a must-read for her fans.

Following the success of "Dear Fatty," French continued to explore the realm of non-fiction with "Me. You. A Diary," released in 2017. This second non-fiction work allowed readers to engage with her thoughts, reflections, and daily musings, offering an intimate look into her world.

However, French's literary talents didn't stop there. She ventured into the world of fiction and authored four novels. "A Tiny Bit Marvelous" (2010), "Oh Dear Silvia" (2012), "According to Yes" (2015), and "Because of You" (2020) showcased her storytelling prowess. "Because of You" even earned the distinction of being shortlisted for the 2021 Women's Prize for Fiction, underscoring her skill as a novelist.

In keeping with her comedic inclinations, French's third non-fiction book, "The Twat Files," is tied to her second stand-up show, "Dawn French is a Huge Twat," and is set to be published in October 2023.

Dawn French's literary contributions are as diverse and captivating as her performances, making her a multifaceted and influential figure in the world of writing as well as entertainment.

INFLUENCE OF ICON

In the realm of comedy and entertainment, Dawn French's remarkable journey has left an indelible mark. From her early days on the comedy circuit to becoming a household name, her career has been nothing short of extraordinary. As we draw the curtain on this exploration of her life and accomplishments, it's evident that her talent transcends boundaries and mediums.

Dawn French's partnership with Jennifer Saunders, a comedic alliance for the ages, has yielded timeless sketches and unforgettable characters. Their collaboration, marked by humor, camaraderie, and wit, will forever be etched in the annals of comedy history.

But French's talents extend far beyond sketch comedy. Her roles on television, stage, and even in the world of literature have showcased her versatility and depth as an artist. Whether she's making us laugh with her unique brand of humor or moving us with her poignant performances, Dawn French is a true virtuoso.

In the realm of writing, French has penned both fiction and non-fiction works, giving readers insight into her world, her thoughts, and her humor. Her books have not only entertained but have also resonated with audiences on a personal level.

Beyond her artistic accomplishments, Dawn French has been a force for good, contributing her time and talent to charitable causes. Her involvement in initiatives like Comic Relief has made a meaningful impact, showcasing her compassion and commitment to making the world a better place.

Awards and recognition have followed her throughout her career, affirming her status as a comedic icon and influential figure. Her accolades are not just acknowledgments of her talent; they are tributes to the joy and laughter she has brought into the lives of countless people.

As we conclude this exploration of Dawn French's life and work, it's clear that her legacy is one of laughter, inspiration, and boundless creativity. Her ability to connect with audiences, both as a performer and as a writer, is a testament to her enduring appeal. In the world of comedy and entertainment, Dawn French's star continues to shine brightly, illuminating our lives with humor, heart, and a touch of magic.

Printed in Great Britain
by Amazon

32719959R00030